Lakes of the Sangres

Atlas of the Sangre de Cristo Mountain Lakes with U.S.G.S. maps and over 200 color photographs

Wojtek Rychlik

Dedicated to my wife,
Barbara, who loves the
Sangres as much as I do.

© 2010 Wojtek Rychlik, Pikes Peak Photo

ISBN Hardcover 978-0-9842554-1-2

ISBN Softcover 978-0-9842554-2-9

Acknowledgements

1. Aerial photography was made
   possible thanks to the courtesy of
   Jack Wojdyla, owner and pilot of
   Cessna 182S airplane.

2. The satellite image source:
   http://earthobservatory.nasa.gov

3. The U.S.G.S. maps are from the U.S.
   Geological Survey.

Lakes of the Sangres

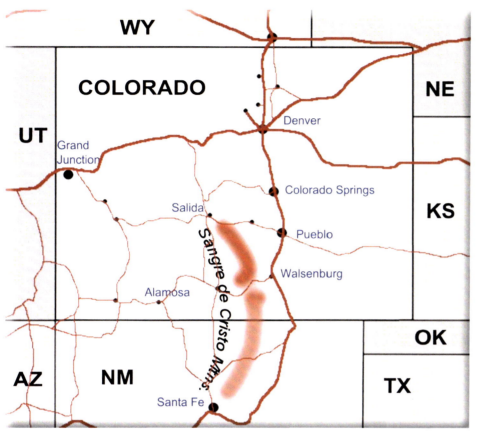

The Sangre de Cristo Mountains, commonly known as the Sangres, are located in the south of Colorado and north New Mexico. This mountain Range is about 200 miles long and spans from Salida, Colorado to Santa Fe, New Mexico. There are ten peaks over 14,000' high in this range, 74 are over 4 km or 13,123' high, and 86 are over 13,000' high. All but three Sangre thirteeners are located in Colorado. This atlas shows all the mountain lakes in a 110 mile-long northern part of the Sangres, in Colorado only.

The atlas is divided by several sections, each begins with a 7.5-minute U.S.G.S. map and a satellite photo with the mapped area marked in yellow, to make localization of the mountains and lakes easier. The images begin from the south on the New Mexico border and continue to the north, ending near Salida. The majority of photographs shown in this atlas were taken in the months of July through September, unless indicated otherwise. There are several geographical names in this book that are not sanctioned by the US Board of Geographical Names, but they are in unofficial use. This is because the Board's current policy effectively prohibits approval of proposed names within wilderness areas that are in local use but not published. Since most of the Sangres are within wilderness boundaries, this policy has resulted in an abundance of unnamed peaks and other geographical features that created confusion amongst hikers or even search rescue teams.

The Wet Mountain Valley and panorama of the Sangres shown below was made in April from an altitude of 12,500' above Highway 96 leading to Westcliffe. It covers all the mountains described in this book. The Spanish Peaks and Culebra range are barely visible on the left. A two-mile long lake on the right of the photo is the De Weese Reservoir.

The State Line Peak Lakes

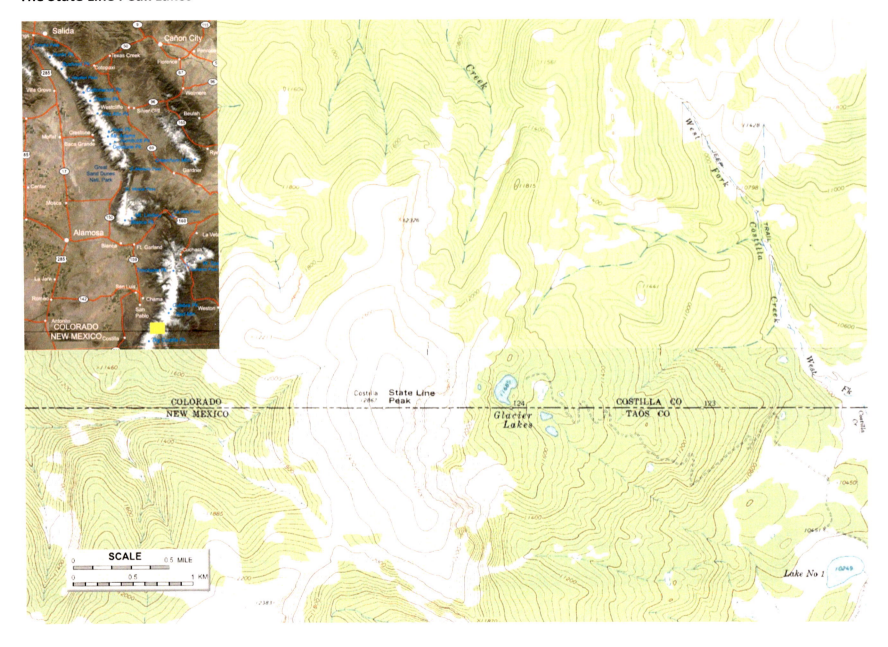

On the Colorado / New Mexico border, there are Glacier Lakes accessible from the east. The Lakes are located east of the State Line Peak. The view from the State Line Peak is to the southeast with the Glacier Lakes behind the Peak. The two smaller lakes belong already to New Mexico. Further away is the New Mexico Lake No. 1.

State Line Peak (12,867') and Glacier Lakes. The largest Glacier Lake is on the left, with an elevation of 11,685', and smaller lakes, with somewhat muddy water, are on the right.

The largest Glacier Lake is on the left, with an elevation of 11,685', and smaller lakes, with somewhat muddy water, are on the right.

Lakes near Culebra Peak

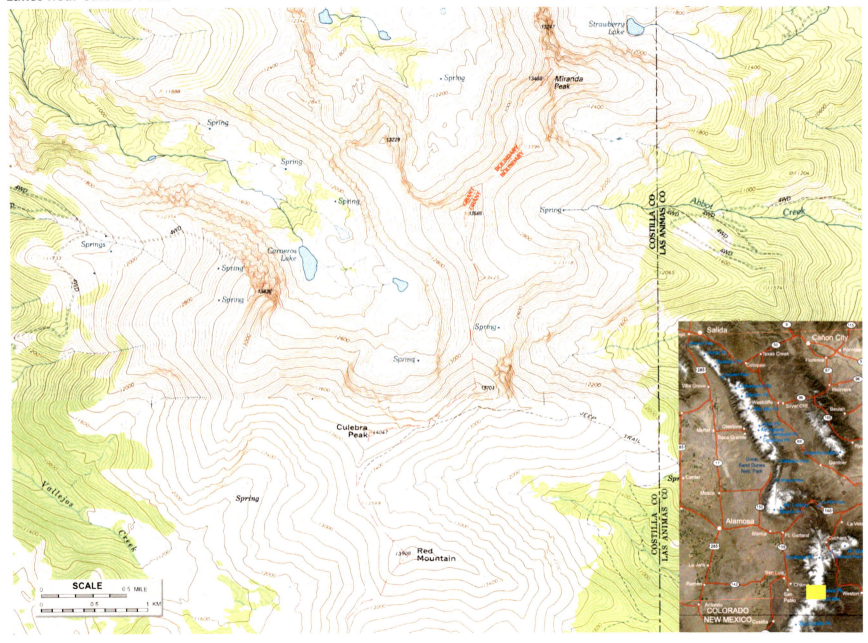

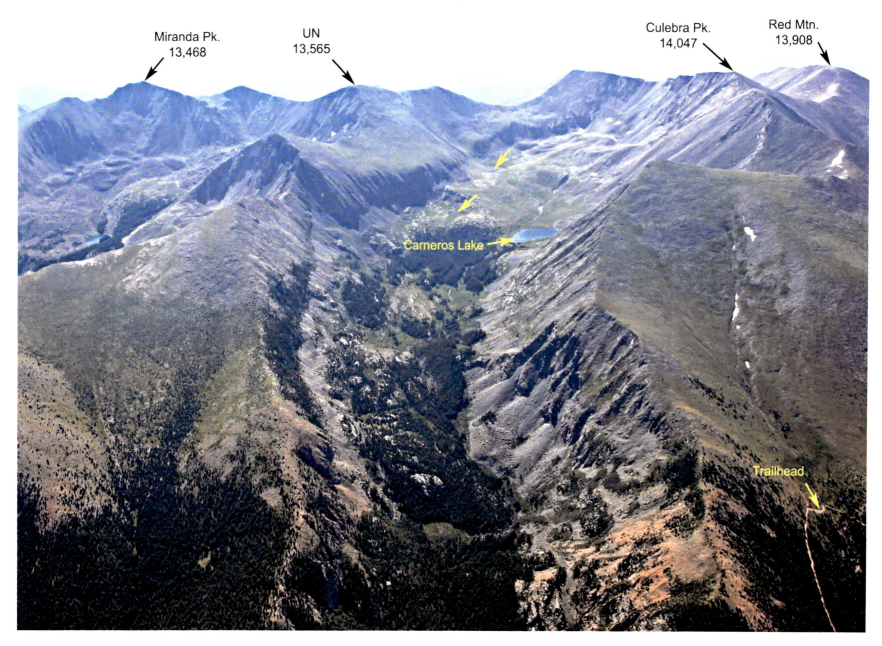

Miranda Pk.
13,468

UN
13,565

Culebra Pk.
14,047

Red Mtn.
13,908

Carneros Lake

Trailhead

Carneros Creek Valley. This photo shows the lakes and the major mountains. The UN 13,565' (UN stands for "Unnamed") is actually a parent of Miranda Peak. A smaller, unnamed lake and pond are marked with arrows. The largest lake is the Carneros Lake (11,900').

A closer view of the Carneros Creek Valley lakes and Culebra Peak. All the mountains that you see here are in private hands. It is possible to hike Culebra Peak but prepare for high fees (check the prices before you decide to go).

Carneros Lake (11,900').

View from the east on the Carneros Creek Valley. Culebra Peak (14,047') is on the left.

A close-up of the Carneros Valley Lakes.

Lakes near Miranda Peak and Lomo Liso Mountain

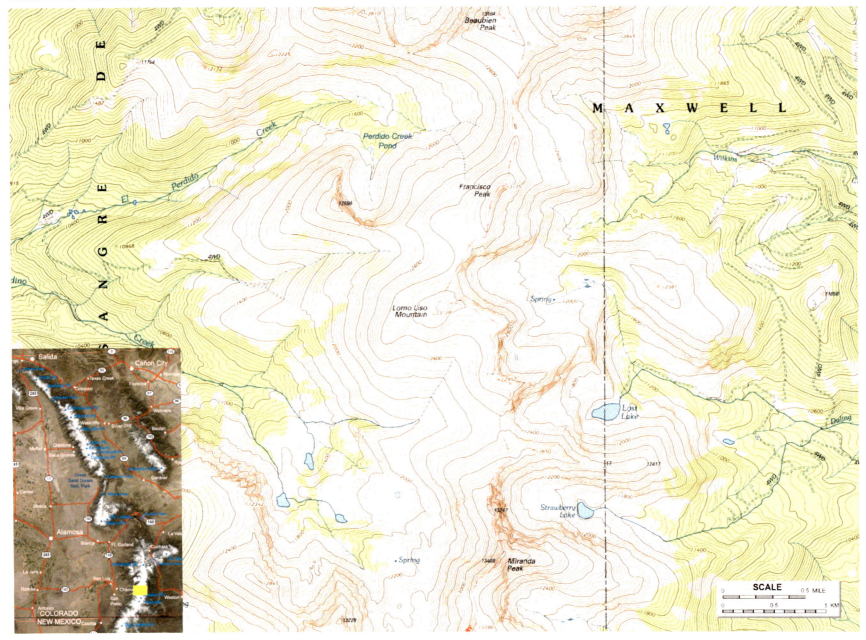

Miranda Pk.
13,468

UN
13,565

"Bernardino Pk."
13,229

Bernardino Creek Valley (west side of Miranda Peak). The yellow arrows point to Miranda Lakes (11300', 11540', 11670', and a pond on 11,860'). Between Miranda Peak and UN 13,565' the prominence is below 300', and therefore, the UN 13,565' is the parent mountain of Miranda Peak. "Bernardino Peak" is a stand-alone peak (prominence larger than 300' between UN 13,565').

13

The lakes in Bernardino Creek Valley (Miranda Lakes) up close, a view from the west.

14

Miranda Lakes up close, view from the east.

Top Miranda Lake.

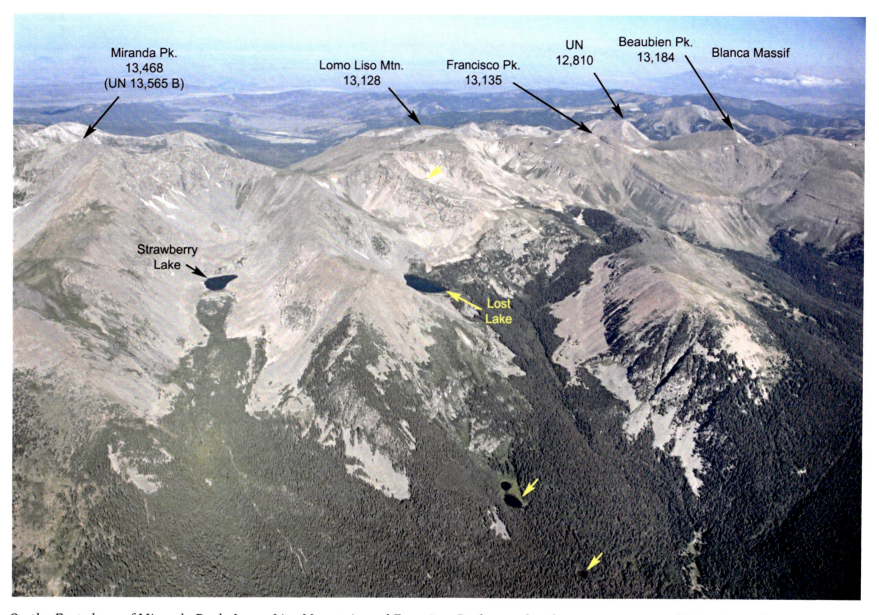

On the East slope of Miranda Peak, Lomo Liso Mountain and Francisco Peak complex there are two named lakes, Strawberry Lake (11,790') and Lost Lake (11,550'). The unnamed ponds below and above the Lost Lake are marked with arrows.

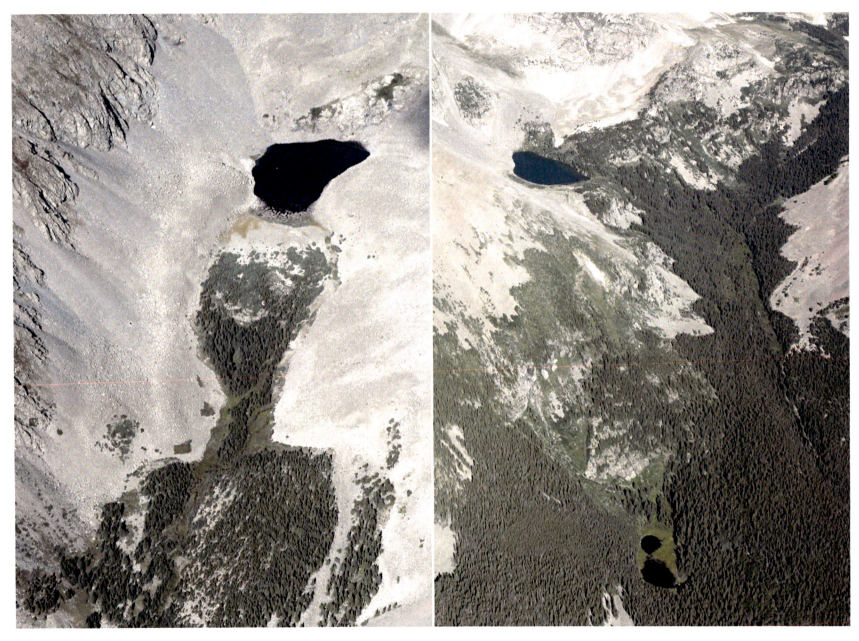

Strawberry Lake (left) and Lost Lake (right), views from the east.

Strawberry Lake (11,790'), view from the north.

Lost Lake (11,550'), southwest view.

Perdido Creek Pond (11,700') is northeast of UN 12,688' and northwest of Francisco Peak. The insert shows a small unnamed pond (12,460') above the Lost Lake, southeast of Lomo Liso Mountain, depicted on page 17.

Lakes near South De Anza Peak

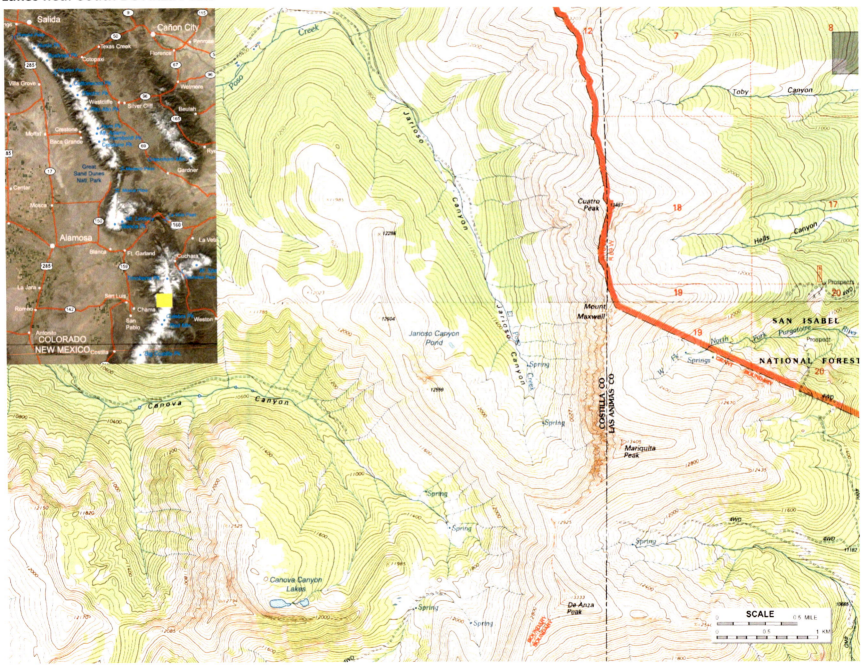

Canova Canyon Lakes (11,790' and 11,850'), view from the north. The UN 12,794' ridge is behind the lakes.

Canova Canyon with UN 12,794', the lakes and the roads. A wide view.

Marquita and De Anza Peaks with a view from the northwest showing Jarioso and Canova Canyons.

Jarioso Canyon Pond (11,750').

Duling Lakes. Two smaller (9750') and the larger lake on the right (9700') are to the east of Miranda Peak, Lomo Liso Mountain, Francisco and Beaubien Peaks. The Lost Lake and Strawberry Lake are barely visible. Insert: Duling Lakes view from a different angle showing additional pond.

Non-alpine lakes east of Miranda Peak. The East South Lake is not marked on the USGS map. The South Lake is at an elevation of 7860' and the Russel Lake at 7796'. Stonewall is the name of a small village.

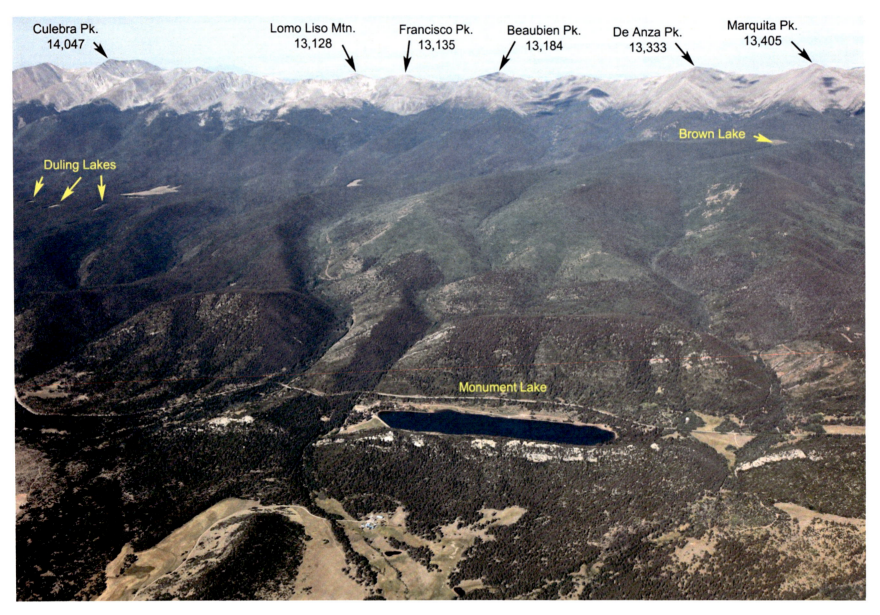

View on the Culebra Range near Monument Lake. The Brown Lake and Duling Lake are barely visible.

Brown Lake (11,100') in October. De Anza Peak (13,333') is on the left and Marquita Peak (13,405') on the right. A 4WD road goes through this lake but all this is on private property. All the land south of Mount Maxwell is private. The west side of Culebra Range is all private land.

North Culebra Range with Cuatro, Trinchera and Teddy's Peaks. Monument Lake (center, 8584') and North Lake (right, 8583'). The Bear and Blue Lakes are hidden behind the UN 11,792'.

North Lake (8583'). The "Unnamed Lake" is not marked on the map and is not visible from Highway 12.

Wolf, Bear, and Blue Lakes. Wolf Lake (11,070'), located below the UN 12,955', is shown as well at the bottom left. All those lakes are in the San Isabel National Forest, and they are the most easily accessible lakes of all the Sangres.

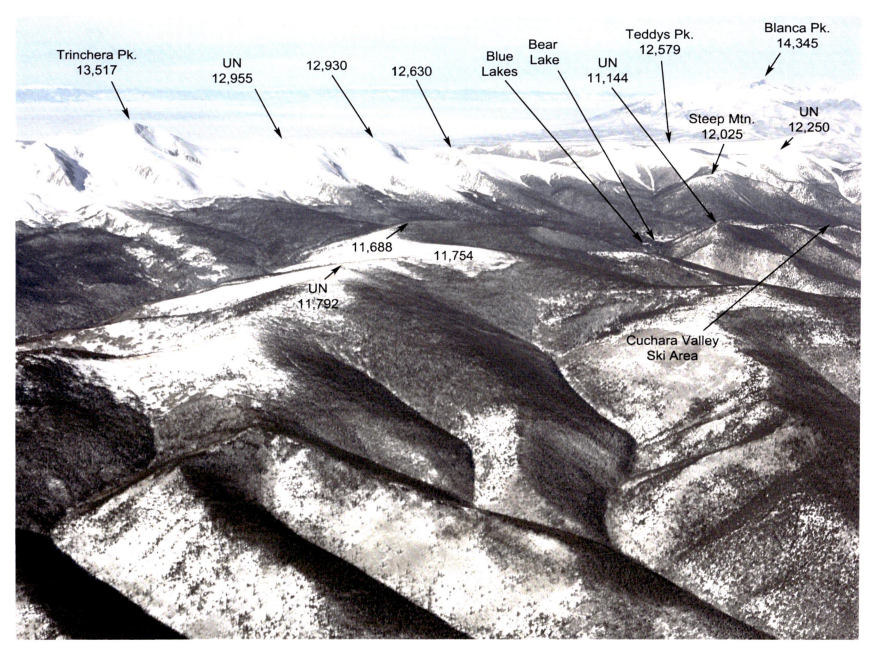

Trinchera Pk.
13,517

UN
12,955

12,930

12,630

Blue
Lakes

Bear
Lake

UN
11,144

Teddys Pk.
12,579

Blanca Pk.
14,345

Steep Mtn.
12,025

UN
12,250

11,688

11,754

UN
11,792

Cuchara Valley
Ski Area

A December view on the north part of Culebra range. Cuchara ski area begins at the far right. The Steep Mountain is easily visible from the Bear Lake.

Bear Lake (far right, 10,430') and the five Blue Lakes in October. The largest Blue Lake is at an elevation of 10, 390'.

Bear Lake (10,430'). The forest-covered Steep Mountain (12,025') is directly behind it, and to the left of the Steep Mountain there is Teddy's Peak (12,579').

A smaller lake downstream of Bear Lake is the Blue Lake number 5 (10,395').

Blue Lake (10, 390'). Below the cloud, is Trinchera Peak (13,517'), the highest in the northern Culebra Range.

A smaller lake downstream of Blue Lake number 1 is Blue Lake number 2 (10,360'), the lowest of all. The Blue Lake number 3 is at an elevation of 10,380'.

On the south slope of West Spanish Peak there is an unnamed lake or reservoir (9325') which is west of Harlick Canyon.

McCarty Park Reservoir (9500') on the North Fork of West Indian Creek (a smaller reservoir is to the north of it, on this picture in the far right). In front, the Raspberry Mountain (11,241') is located approximately 2 miles northwest of Cuchara.

Blanca Massif - Lakes South of Ellingwood Peak

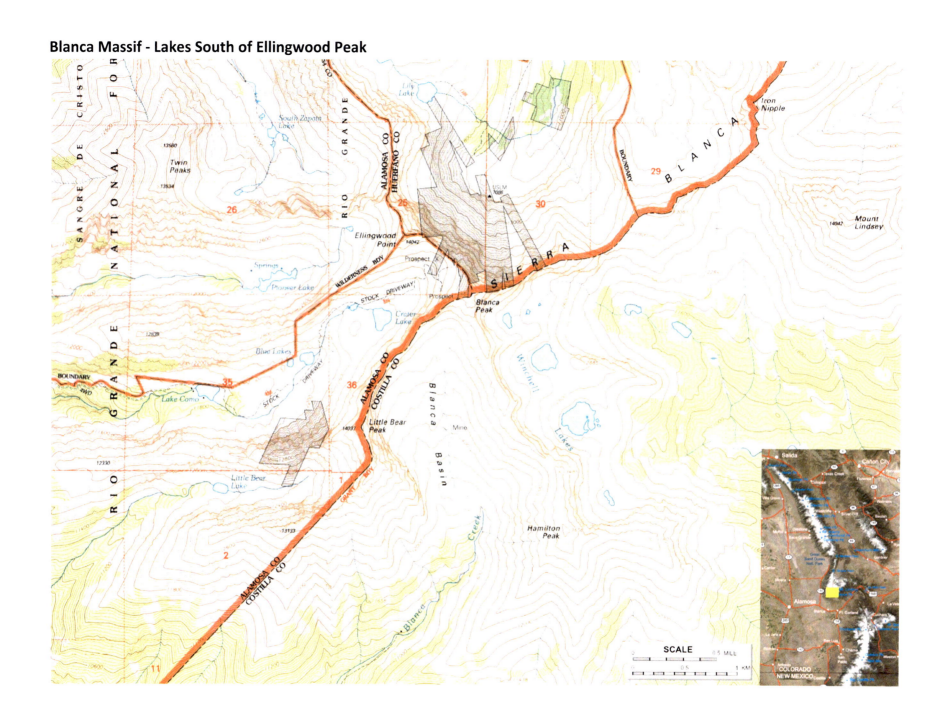

SCALE

Trail to Blanca Peak (lakes on the left) and to the Little Bear Lake. The short arrows point to smaller unnamed lakes and ponds.

Little Bear Lake (11,900'). Views from the west (left photo) and southwest with the Little Bear Peak, 14,037', behind (right).

Como Lake (11,750'). It is the most popular campsite on the trail to Blanca Peak. From the National Forest boundary to Lake Como is 4.2 miles and about 3000' up. From the Lake to Blanca Peak is another 3.2 miles, and another 2600' uphill.

Blue Lakes of Blanca Massif. Elevation of the larger lake is 12,150'.

Crater Lake (12,700') is the top lake on the trail to Blanca Peak and Ellingwood Point.

A wider view on the Holbrook Creek Valley. This photo shows the ridge between Little Bear (right, 14,037') and Blanca Peaks (14,345'). Ellingwood Point (14,042') is to the left of Blanca Peak. The Little Bear Lake is on the right.

On the bottom left there is a pond (12,810') below Ellingwood Point. Behind this mountain, there is Huerfano Peak on the left (labeled also as Ute Peak in some maps, 13,828') and Mount Lindsey (14,042') to the right of it. On the bottom right, you can see the Crater Lake in front of Blanca Peak.

50

Pioneer Lake (12,050') is located below the Ellingwood Point.

The Winchell Lakes (pointed by the yellow arrows) are one of the most picturesque lakes of the Sangres, but at the same time, one of the least accessible. Hamilton Peak is partially obscured by the clouds. The Lily Lakes are to the right of Blanca Peak.

The top Winchell Lakes. Their elevation is 13,100', 12,750' (2nd largest) and 12,350' (the largest). The 4th smallest lake in this row is at an elevation of 12,310'. The Lily Lakes are at the top right of this photo.

The top Winchell Lake (13,100'). The Twin Peaks are behind Blanca Peak.

The second highest and the second largest Winchell Lake (12,750'). The second lowest Winchell Lake is in the background. An old gold mine is at the bottom left.

The largest Winchell Lake (12,350').

The two lowest Winchell Lakes at elevations of 11,460' and 11,630'.

Blanca Massif - Lakes North of Ellingwood Peak

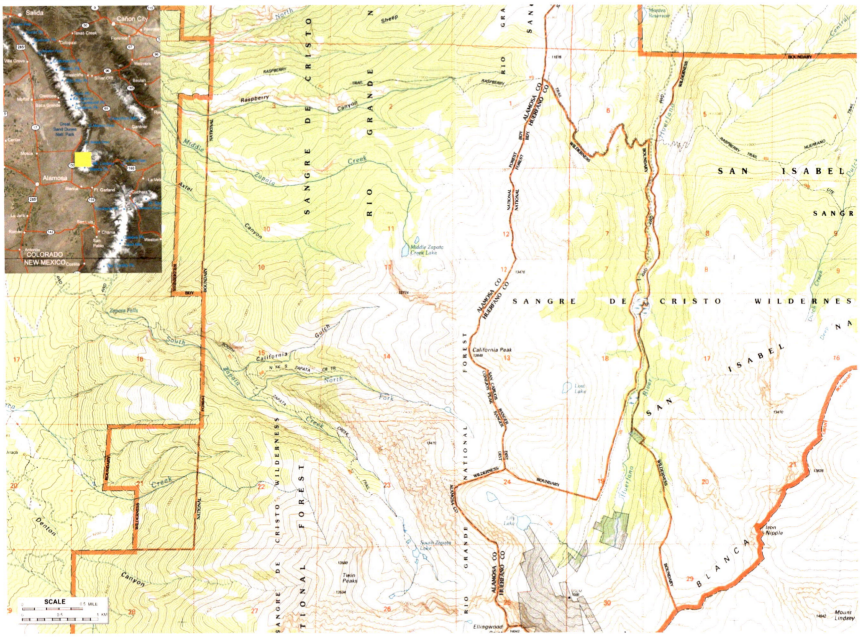

Huerfano Basin lakes: the Lily and Lost Lakes. Only the North Twin Peak is visible here. The "Lily Peak" and California Peak are on the west side of Huerfano Basin, and the Huerfano Peak and Iron Nipple are on the east side of the Basin. In the San Luis Valley, behind the peaks, you can see the San Luis Lake (not an alpine lake but a San Luis Valley Lake, 7519') in the San Luis Lakes State Wildlife Refuge.

Lily Lakes, a view from the east. They are at elevation of 12,350' and 12,630'. The trail to the Lake is relatively short (3.2 miles), easy (1700' up) and beautiful. Try when aspens rich their peak colors.

Lily Lakes, view from the northwest.

Lower Lily Lake. Large rocks, hard to get through, surround both Lily Lakes. The Iron Nipple is in the extreme left, followed by Mount Lindsey.

South Zapata Lake (11,900'). View from the north, showing South Zapata Top Pond at an elevation of 12,520'. From the Zapata Falls Trailhead to the Lake there is 4.5 miles and a 2600' climb. Then, you may climb the Twin Peaks.

The Lost Lake (12,260') of Blanca Massif is located on the east-facing slope of California Peak.

Lost Lake of Blanca Massif, a broader view. Blanca Peak is on the right, and Hamilton Peak is behind it, to the left.

The Middle Zapata Creek Lake (13,849') is on the northwest slope of California Peak. You can also see the Lost Lake on the other side of this mountain.

Middle Zapata Creek Lake (11,790').

Montez Reservoir (10,420'). The road to Lily Lakes Trailhead is at the top of the photo.

Lakes of Mount Herrad (Mount Seven) Massif

Medano Lake and the east slope of Mount Herrad. Behind the mountain you can see the Great Sand Dunes in the San Luis Valley.

Medano Lake (Main, 11,500'), view from above Mount Herrad, formerly known as Mount Seven. From the Medano Lake Trailhead (less than a mile away to the northwest of Medano Pass) there is a 3.5 mile hike, 1900' uphill.

The North Medano Lake (11,650') is in the northeast of "Medano Peak", part of which is visible here on the bottom right.

Hudson Branch Lake (11,980'). The bottom left summit is the "Hudson Branch Peak" (12,883').

A closer view of the Hudson Branch Lakes.

The Smith Creek, northwest of Mount Herrad, begins from the Smith Lake (11,620'). The water flows to the Sand Creek Valley. View from the north.

A broader view of the Smith Lake area from the northwest. The mountain on the left is "Medano Peak" and Mount Herrad is on the right.

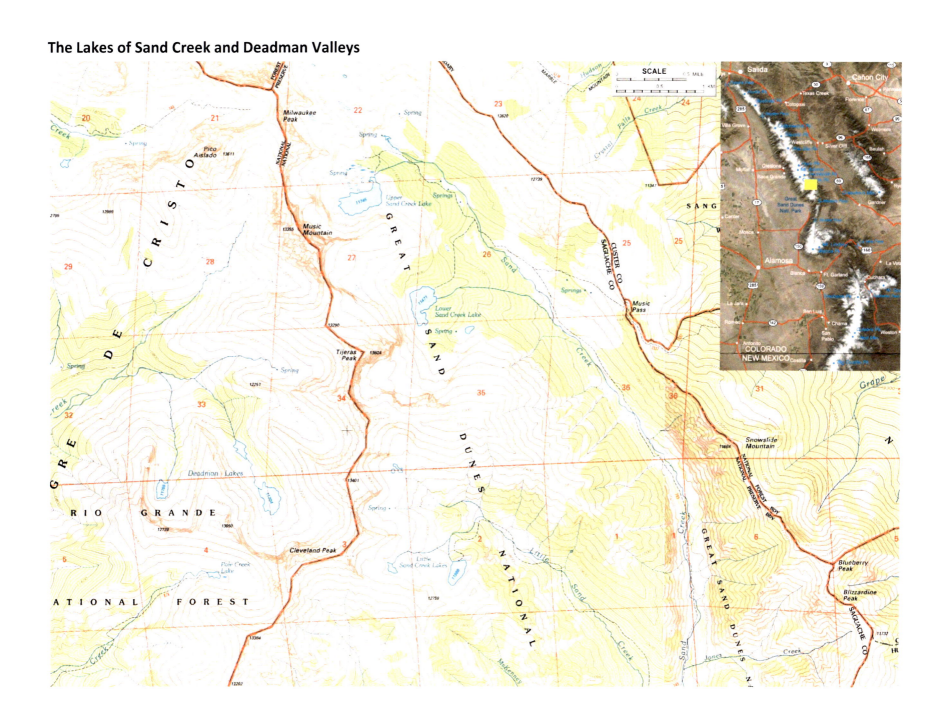

West view on the Sand Creek Valley. The South end of Marble Mountain, at the top left, slopes down to Music Pass. The ridge continues through the Snowslide Mountain and Blueberry Peak, with its west end called the Blizzardine Peak. The top of the "Hudson Branch Peak" is not visible but you can see its North slope with the 12,195' summit. The most massive mountain that you see when standing on Music Pass is a 13,369' sub-summit of Tijeras Peak. A really steep trail through the Little Sand Creek Basin leads to the Little Sand Creek Lakes.

78

Lower Little Sand Creek Lake (11,988'), view from the northeast. The top of the mountain in the foreground is a 13,495' sub-summit of Tijeras Peak, the northwest edge of the Little Sand Creek Basin.

View of the Lower Little Sand Creek Lake from the northwest. It's a beautiful location, but a strenuous uphill (800'), downhill (1700') and again uphill (2300') hike of 8.5 miles-long from the Upper Music Pass Trailhead makes this site infrequently visited. Appropriate for an at least two-day out-and-back trip.

Little Sand Creek Basin. Little Sand Creek Lakes are on the left (the Upper Lake is at 12,580'), and Little Sand Creek Ponds (upper-right center, 12,220') are below the UN 13,401' and the 13,495' sub-summit of Tijeras Peak.

Close-up of the Little Sand Creek Ponds.

Sand Creek Lakes. The Lower Lake (11,471') is below Tijeras Peak (13,604') on the left, and the Upper Lake (11,745') is on the right. Above the Upper Sand Creek Lake is Music Mountain (13,355') and behind this mountain you can see a part of the Deadman Valley.

Lower Sand Creek Lake (11,471'). It is one of the easiest and shortest backpack trails in the Sangres. The trail is about 3.1 miles from the Music Pass Trailhead, that goes 800' uphill to Music Pass, 400' downhill to the Sand Creek and 500' uphill to the Lake.

Upper Sand Creek Lake (11,745'). Photo taken from the ground in October. It is relatively easy to get to from the Music Pass Trailhead (3.5 miles), with only a 300' higher climb than to the Lower Sand Creek Lake.

The southwest view of the Upper Sand Creek Lake (11,745') with all the Upper Sand Creek Ponds near the Lake.

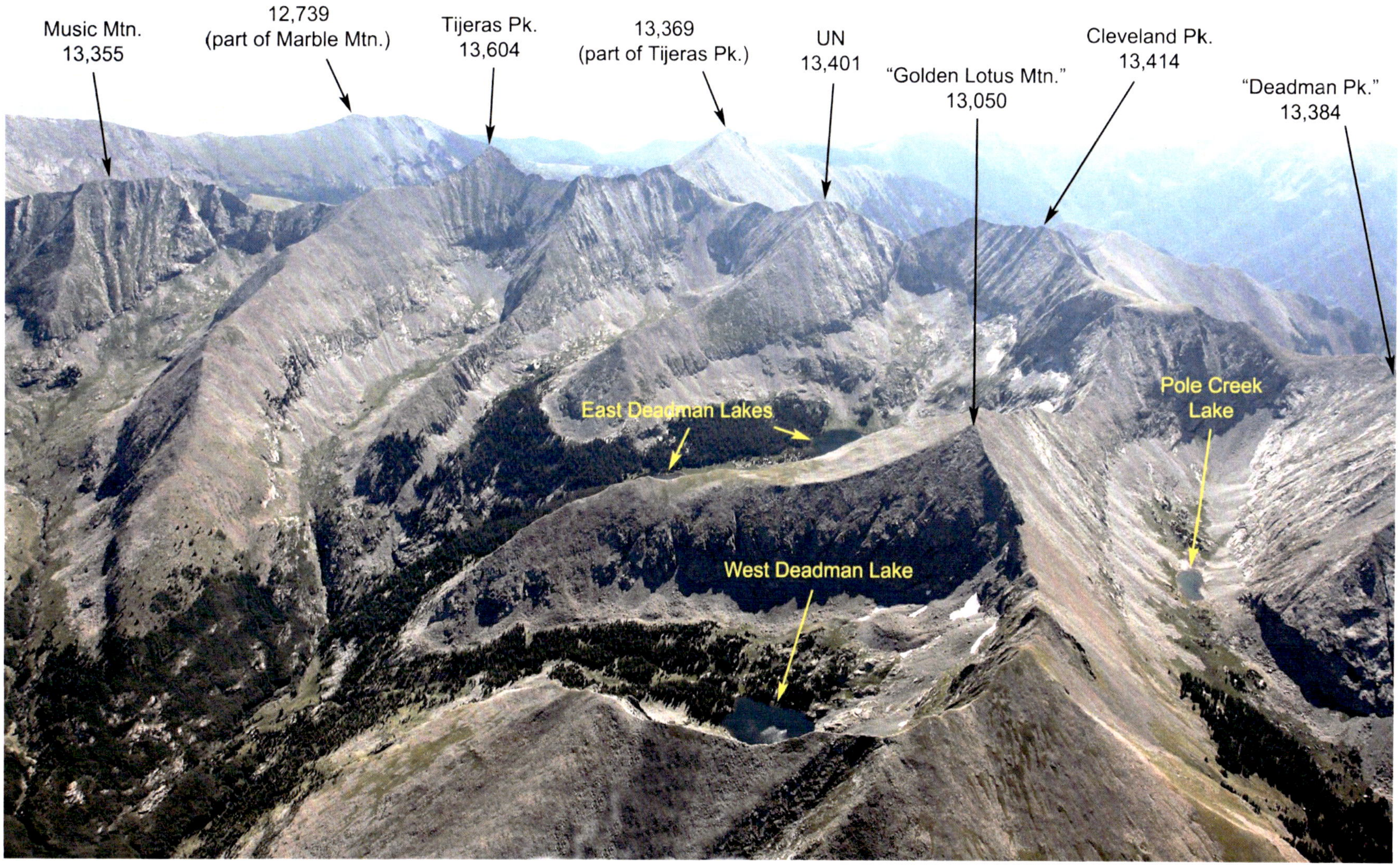
Music Mtn.
13,355
12,739
(part of Marble Mtn.)
Tijeras Pk.
13,604
13,369
(part of Tijeras Pk.)
UN
13,401
"Golden Lotus Mtn."
13,050
Cleveland Pk.
13,414
"Deadman Pk."
13,384
East Deadman Lakes
Pole Creek
Lake
West Deadman Lake

The Deadman Valley with all its lakes: two East and one West Deadman Lakes. The Pole Creek Lake is in a separate Pole Creek drainage. Mountains depicted here are the Music Mountain, Tijeras Peak, UN 13,401', "Golden Lotus Mountain" and Cleveland Peak. Partially visible here are the Marble Mountain and "Deadman Peak". *Note:* some hikers call "Deadman Peak" the "Golden Lotus Mountain". Both names are not sanctioned by the USGS Board, despite that the Golden Lotus Mountain name has been in print on several map editions.

East Deadman Lakes. The Lower Little Sand Creek Lake is visible in the top right and Tijeras Peak is in the top left. There is a trail to the Deadman Lakes but because it's not maintained and seldom used (especially after establishing the Great Sand Dunes National Park and shortening the drivable road), you may get lost. Do not try this one alone.

The East Deadman Lakes (11,650' and 11,704') resemble a little bear chasing its mama.

Upper East Deadman Lake (11,704').

Lower East Deadman Lake (11,650').

All the Deadman Lakes and Pole Creek Lake. The closest to the viewer is the West Deadman Lake (11,765'). Golden Lotus Mountain (13,050') is in the center.

A view from above the West Deadman Lake (11,765').

Pole Creek Lake (11,980').

Cottonwood and South Colony Creeks Valleys

The Cottonwood Creek Valley ends with the Milwaukee Peak. The Lower Cottonwood Lake is behind the 12,751' sub-summit of UN 13,020'. The Pond marked at bottom right is at an elevation of 11,860'.

Cottonwood Lakes. The top lake is barely visible as a dark line in the upper left.

Lower Cottonwood Lake (11,810').

Cottonwood Lake (12,310'). Crestone Needle is behind it and the mountain on the right is called "Crestolita". There is a 4.5-mile trail to the lake from the Cottonwood Trailhead near Baca Grande (almost 4000' vertical).

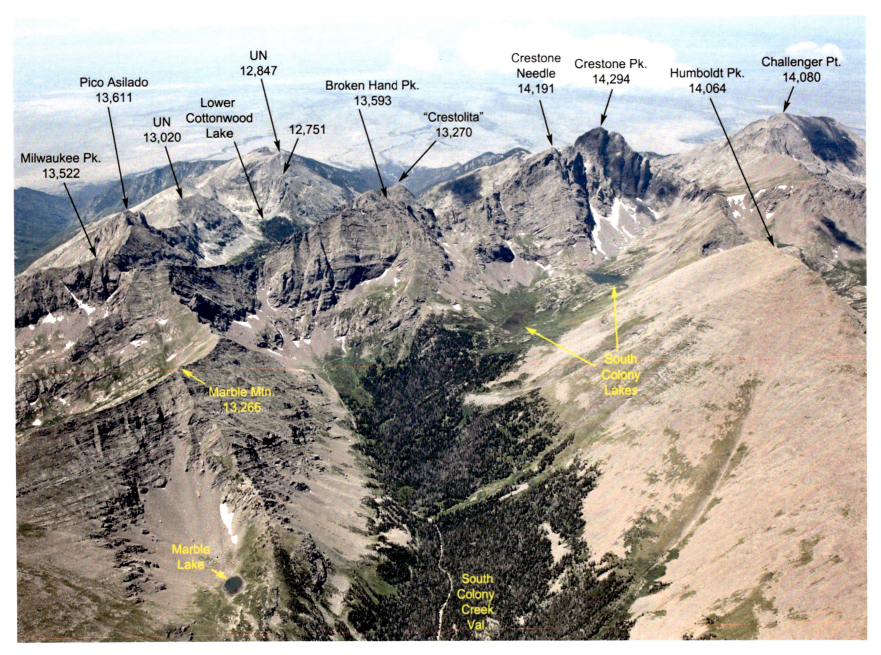

Milwaukee Pk.
13,522

Pico Asilado
13,611

UN
13,020

Lower
Cottonwood
Lake

UN
12,847

12,751

Broken Hand Pk.
13,593

"Crestolita"
13,270

Crestone
Needle
14,191

Crestone Pk.
14,294

Humboldt Pk.
14,064

Challenger Pt.
14,080

Marble Mtn
13,266

South
Colony
Lakes

Marble
Lake

South
Colony
Creek
Val.

South Colony Creek Valley with South Colony Lakes and Marble Lake. Before the road closure in the fall of 2009 it was the most frequently visited part of the Sangres.

The Marble Lake (11,700') is basically a shallow pond. On the right, a former trailhead to the South Colony Lakes.

South Colony Lakes with Crestone Needle summit in the bottom right. The lakes look close to each other, but it's over a one-mile hike.

Lower South Colony Lake (11,670') and several ponds on the east and west sides. View from the Humboldt Peak angle (from the south). It used to be only a 1.5 mile hike and just about 600' elevation change. Since 2010, it is 4 miles and 1000' more to climb. The decision to shorten the road was based on environmental issues.

View from the ground on the Lower South Colony Lake and Milwaukee Peak.

South Colony Lakes (11,670' and 12,030'), view from the east. The Crestone Needle is in the foreground of Crestone Peak.

Upper South Colony Lake with a trail leading to Humboldt Peak.

View of the Upper South Colony Lake from the ground.

North Colony Lakes

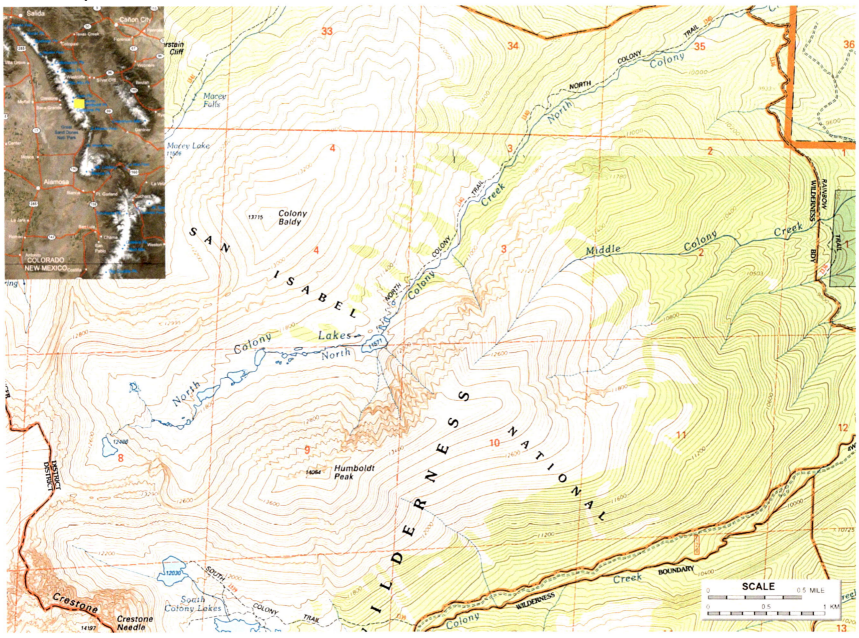

North Colony Lakes and many ponds, viewed from the west. The Bench Lake is at the bottom left. In the upper left, Colony Baldy Mountain and South Macey and Lower Macey Lakes. The trail to the Humboldt Peak is clearly visible at the bottom right.

The North Colony Lakes are indicated by the yellow arrows. View from the east. The shortest access to the lakes is from the South Colony Road. Park your car near the Rainbow Trail and hike 7.5 miles (to the first lake there is over 1800' elevation change, and to Bench Lake is nearly 2800') to the last Lake excluding the Bench Lake. You may add two more miles of a hike by starting the trip at the Horn Creek Trailhead, but the path to only the Macey Lakes Trail through the Rainbow Trail is long enough to get bored.

The Lower North Colony lakes viewed from the west in October. The lowest large lake (top right) is at an elevation of 11,571'. The lake at the bottom of this picture is at an elevation of 11,750'.

A close up of the Bench Lake (12,486'). The North Colony Creek starts at this lake. View from the west, the Bear's Playground angle.

The Bench Lake is the top lake of the North Colony Creek Valley. The Bear's Playground, partially seen here, is above the Lake to the right and the "Colony Ridge" (part of Crestone Peak) is on the left.

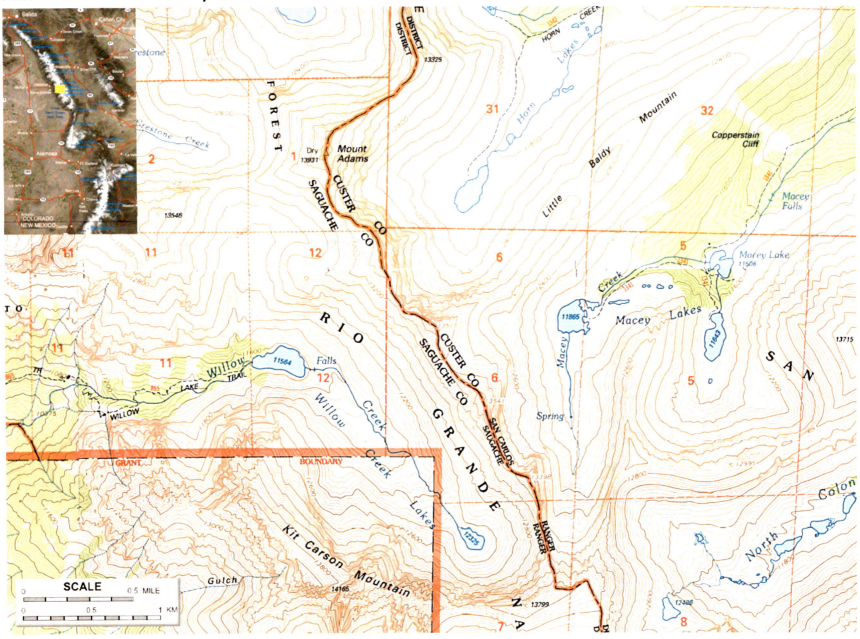

Little Horn Pk.
13,143

Mt. Adams
13,931

Little Baldy Mtn. "Horn Lakes Wall"
12,982   13,530

13,517

UN
13,541

Colony Baldy
13,705

"Willow Peak"
13,546

13,005

Challenger Pt.
14,081

13,151

Lower Willow Lake (11,564') and the mountains surrounding the valley. This is one of the most picturesque lake of the Sangres. The trail from the South Crestone Trailhead near Crestone is only 5 miles long, but nearly 2700' uphill, and that makes it quite strenuous. It's a great place to camp and continue another 2 miles with the same elevation change to rich the Challenger Point summit or 2.6 miles to rich the Kit Carson Mountain summit on the next day.

Willow Creek Valley with the Lower and Upper Willow Lakes. The Lakes are about a mile from each other, with the elevation difference of nearly 800'.

Upper Willow Lake (12,325'), with the surrounding mountains: Challenger Point, Kit Carson Mountain, Columbia Point, and "Obstruction Peak". Crestone Peak is at the top right.

A close-up of the Lower Willow Lake. There are waterfalls above and below the Lake.

Macey Lakes. It is a 7 miles hike from the Horn Creek Trailhead, with a 2500' elevation change to the Upper Lake. Half of this distance is on a relatively flat Rainbow Trail.

Upper Macey Lake (left, 11,865') and Middle (or South) Macey Lake (right, 11,647').

Upper Macey Lake (11,865′).

Middle (South) Macey Lake (11,647') and the Lower Macey Lake on the left. The Middle Lake is on a trail to Colony Baldy, from which, there is a little over 2000 vertical feet to reach the summit.

The Lower Macey Lake (11,506') is on the right, and the South Macey Lake (11,647') is on the left.

A closer view of the Lower Macey Lake. That's the best of the three lakes to camp nearby.

Horn, Dry and Crestone Lakes

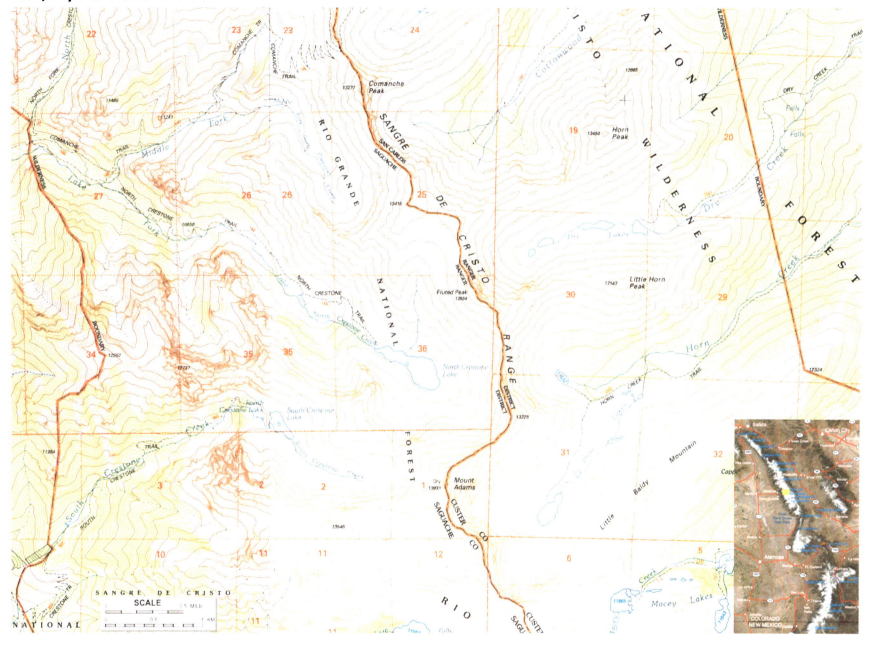

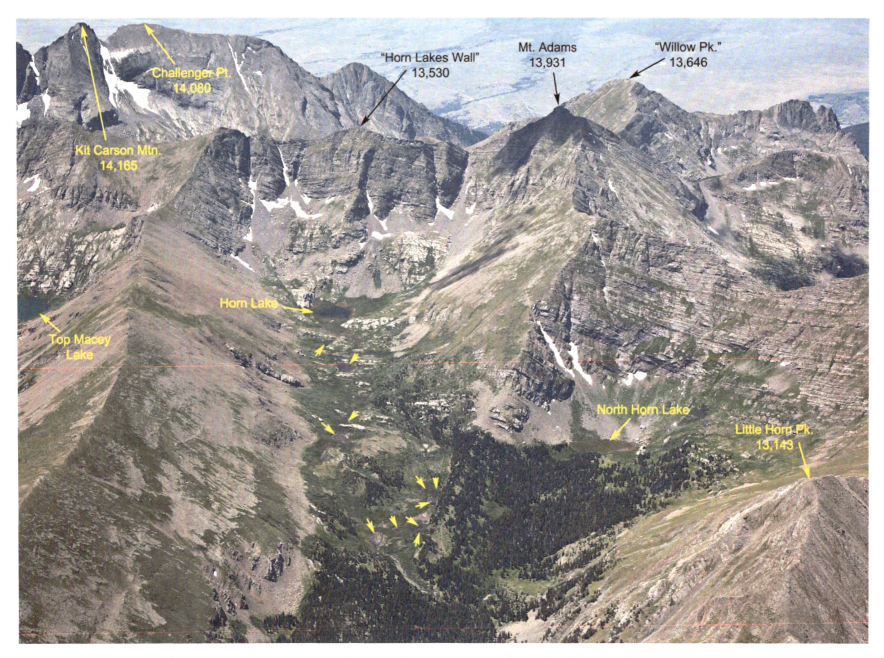

Horn Lakes. The unmarked arrows are pointing to the Horn Ponds. Historically, Columbia and Challenger Points belong to Kit Carson Mountain, however, the prominences of the Points are over 300', and according to the peak definition in Colorado the lower two Points are, in fact, independent peaks.

126

The Top Horn Lake (11,830') view from the west. The trail to this lake is 5.5 miles long and begins at the Horn Creek Trailhead. The elevation difference is 2500', but the views are great and the slope is not too bad (except about a mile before the lakes), so it doesn't feel that much strenuous as the trail to the adjacent Dry or Macey Lakes.

The Horn Lake view from the east.

Lower Horn Ponds.

North Horn Lake (11,632'), view from the north. The Lower Horn Ponds are in the top left.

A general view on the Macey and Horn Lakes, separated by the Little Baldy Mountain.

Four Dry Lakes (see the yellow arrows) are surrounded by the Little Horn Peak from the south, Fluted Peak from the west and Horn Peak from the north.

The two lowest Dry Lakes (11,820' and 11,860') with the Little Horn Peak in the background. A trail from the Horn Creek Trailhead to the Lowest Lake is 4.2 miles long and 2500' uphill. Add only another 100 vertical feet and 0.8 mile to the Top Lake. The trail is strenuous due to a relatively high slope before it reaches the first lake.

The top Dry Lakes (11,940' and 11,950') and Fluted Peak. Although not described anywhere, it seems plausible to climb on the Horn Peak – Fluted Peak ridge to a shallow grassy area depicted here in upper right (elevation slightly below 13,300'), from which there is less than a mile away and about 1500' down to one of the most impressive lakes of the Sangres, the North Crestone Lake.

The top Dry Lakes view from the ground showing the impressive Fluted Peak (13,554') behind them.

The North Crestone Creek Valley is surrounded by several mountains, depicted here. The North Crestone Lake ends this impressive-looking, full of aspens valley. The trail to the Lake from the west side of the Sangres, North Crestone Trailhead, is 6 miles long and 3300' uphill – about the same in length than the route through the Dry Lakes, described on page 134, but less challenging.

North Crestone Lake (11,780'). Behind the unnamed mountain, UN 13,153', is the partially visible South Crestone Lake.

North Crestone Lake surrounded by Fluted Peak on the right and Mount Adams on the left. The UN 13,153' is in the foreground (smooth round western slope), and Horn Peak is at the top left.

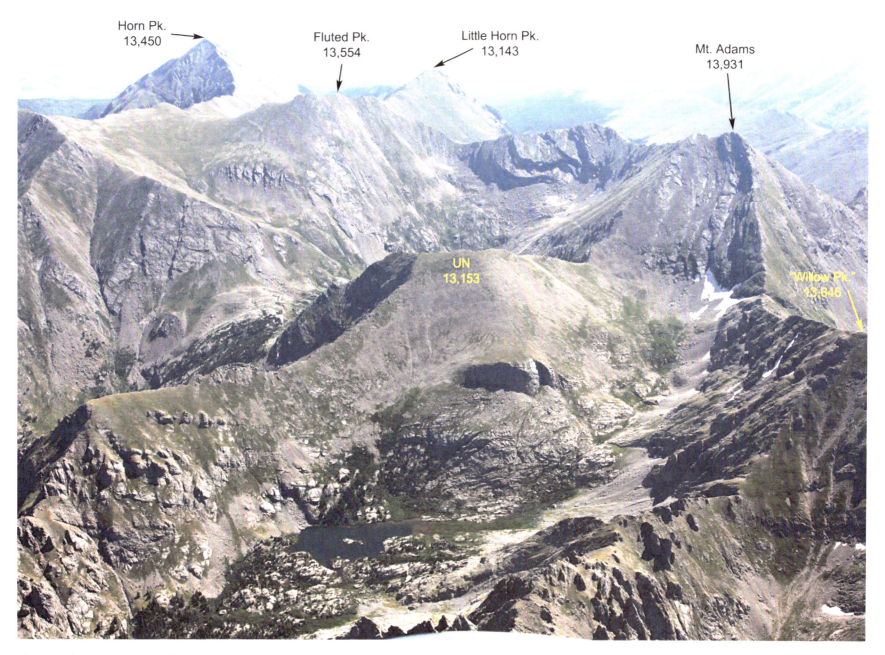

The South Crestone Creek Valley is surrounded by the UN 13,153', Mount Adams and "Willow Peak". The North Crestone Lake is hidden behind the UN 13,153'.

South Crestone Lake (11,780'), view from the west. The trail to this lake starts at the South Crestone Trailhead and is 5.5 miles long with a 3000' elevation change. It is attractive, with nice views on the San Luis Valley and impressive rock formations.

South Crestone Lake (11,780').

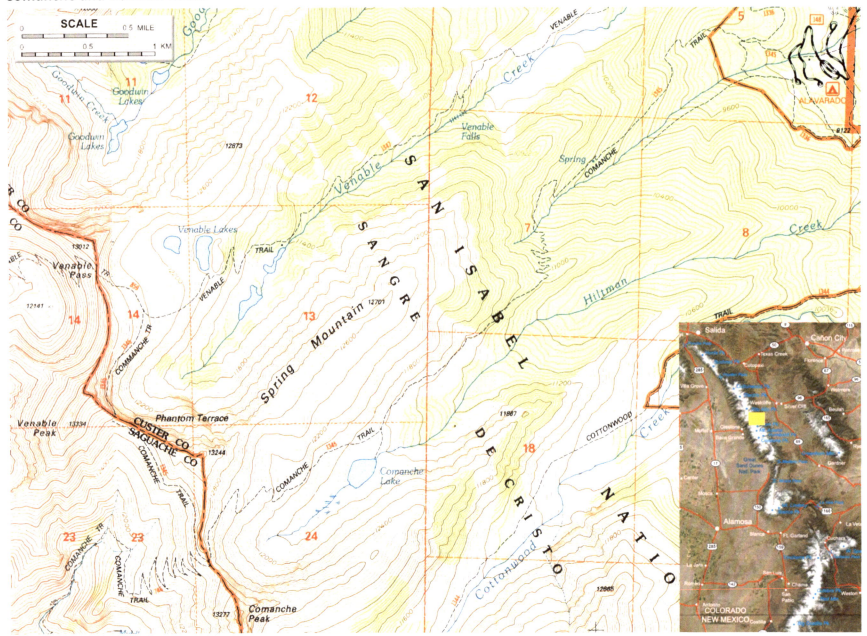

Comanche Lake (11,670'), view from the west. To the right of it, there is a higher, shallow but large lake at 11,700' that is not marked on the USGS map. Comanche Peak is on the right and the Spring Mountain is on the left.

Venable (left) and Comanche Lakes, view from the west. Spring Mountain is in the center. There is 4.5 miles (elevation change 2600') from the Venable-Comanche trailhead to the Comanche Lake. The trail continues uphill another 1100' around the Spring Mountain on the west-facing slope and leads through the Phantom Terrace to Venable Lakes (Venable-Comanche Loop Trail, about 3 miles-long). More on page 147.

Comanche Lake is the lower lake depicted here. The Phantom Terrace (see the insert) on Venable Peak is part of the trail leading from Venable Lakes to Comanche Lake.

Venable Lakes (11,990' and 12,070'). Venable Peak (13,334') is at the top center, and Venable Pass is to the right. Spring Mountain is on the left.

Venable Lakes view from the west. The trail on the left leads through the Venable Pass, and the trail on the right, through the Phantom Terrace. The trail from the Venable-Comanche Trailhead to the Lower Venable Lake is 4.2 miles long with 2900' elevation change, and than up another 800' to the top of the Phantom Terrace and then down 1100' to Comanche Lake (see p. 144), so that the round trip through the Venable-Comanche Loop Trail and back to the Venable-Comanche Trailhead is about 12 miles.

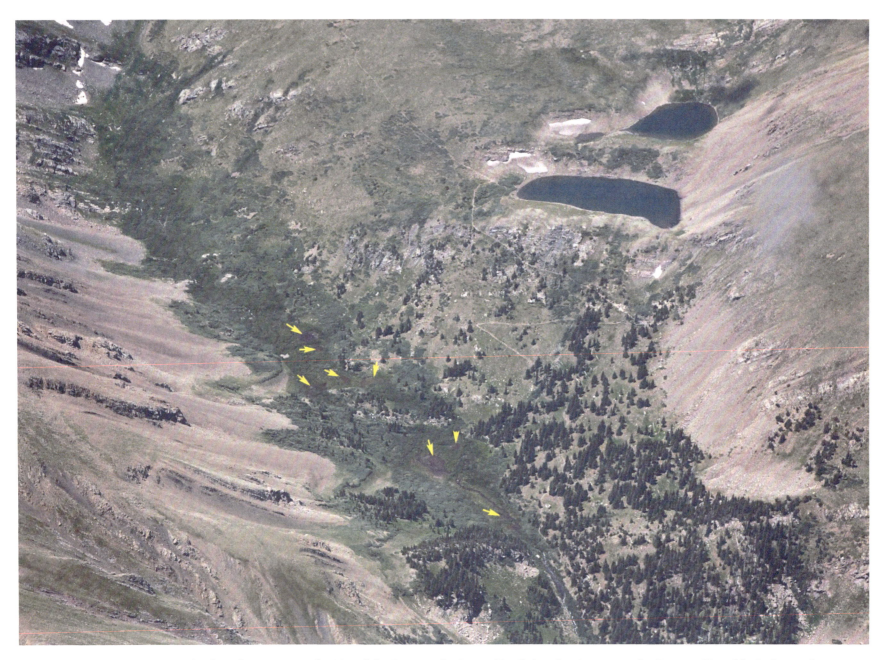

The Venable Ponds are marked with arrows. The Venable-Comanche Loop Trail that begins near the Lower Venable Lake and continues upwards and to the left is clearly visible.

Goodwin Lakes

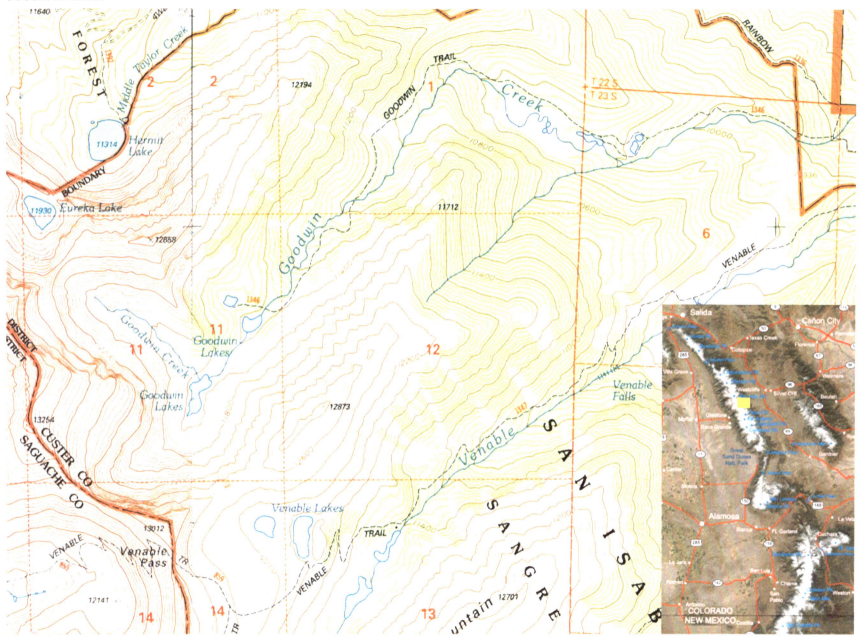

Top of the Goodwin Creek Valley. Three arrows point to the Goodwin Lakes.

View of the bottom two Goodwin Lakes. The large one is at an elevation of 11,390' and the North Lake is at 11,460'.

Upper Goodwin Lake (left, 11,580') in October. On the right, the entire valley viewed from the west. It is a moderate hike. From the Venable-Comanche Trailhead to the Upper Goodwin Lake is 5 miles (2500' vertical), and 1.5 miles of which is on a relatively horizontal Rainbow Trail.

View from the west on Goodwin Lakes. The Top Lake is at an elevation of 11,580'. The view is more impressive than this one when you hike near the Upper Lake.

Elaine, Rito Alto and San Isabel Lakes

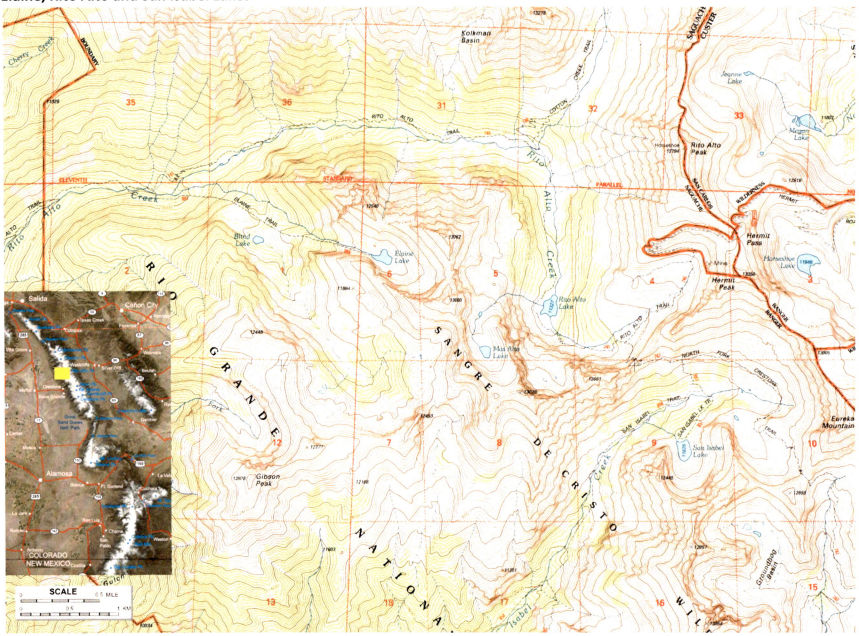

154

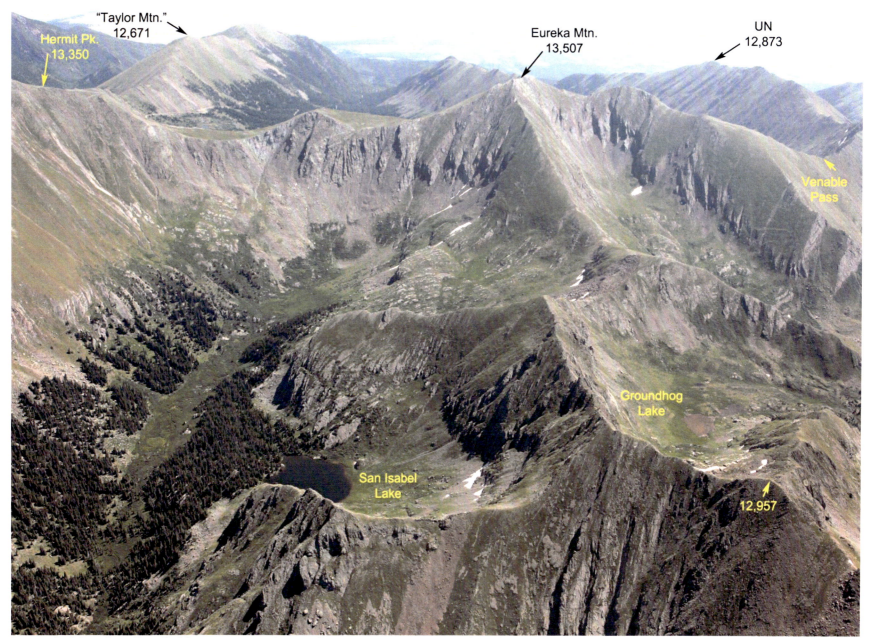

San Isabel Creek Valley (left). Hermit Peak, Eureka Mountain, UN 12,873', and Venable Pass are at the top. Accessible from the west, San Isabel Trailhead starts at the end of the County Road 66-T, and ends at the San Isabel Lake. It is a strenuous, 5.5 miles long, trail with a 3400' elevation change.

12,957

Pyramid Mtn.
13,054

Groundhog Basin with Groundhog Lake (11,850'). Venable Pass (12,600') is on the top right. The Groundhog Basin is accessible through Venable Pass (1200' down and nearly 500' up) or from the North Crestone Trailhead through the North Fork Trail (5 miles, and vertical 3400').

San Isabel Lake (11,625') is also accessible from Venable Pass (about 4 miles and very strenuous hike: 800' down, 700' up, 900' down and 200' up).

Alto Massif Lakes. This part of the Mountains is not well known because they are not easily accessible. To reach the Rito Alto Lake from the west, start from the Rito Alto Trailhead and walk 6.5 miles (3000' vertical). Page 160 describes a shorter alternative trail to the Rito Alto Lake.

Mas Alto Lake (12,460'). The Mas Alto Pond is located below it, to the left. There is no described trail to this lake, but it may be approached from the Rito Alto Lake by an over 1100' rough climb.

Rito Alto Lake (11,327'). View from the west on the Hermit Pass (13,045'). The Hermit Pass trail is clearly visible on the top. The insert is the Lake photo made from the north direction. This is the easiest lake within this lake group to reach because of the proximity to the Hermit Pass (an over 2-mile downhill hike, vertically 1700') that can be reached by a motor vehicle.

160

Elaine Lake (11,700'), view from the west. From the Rito Alto Trailhead it is a strenuous 4.5 miles hike with an elevation gain of 3400', but considering beauty of this lake, it is well worth the effort.

Alto Peak Massif, view from the north.

The Blind Lake (10,820') may be reached from the Elaine Lake Trail.

Hermit Pass (Middle Taylor Creek Valley) and North Taylor Creek Valley Lakes

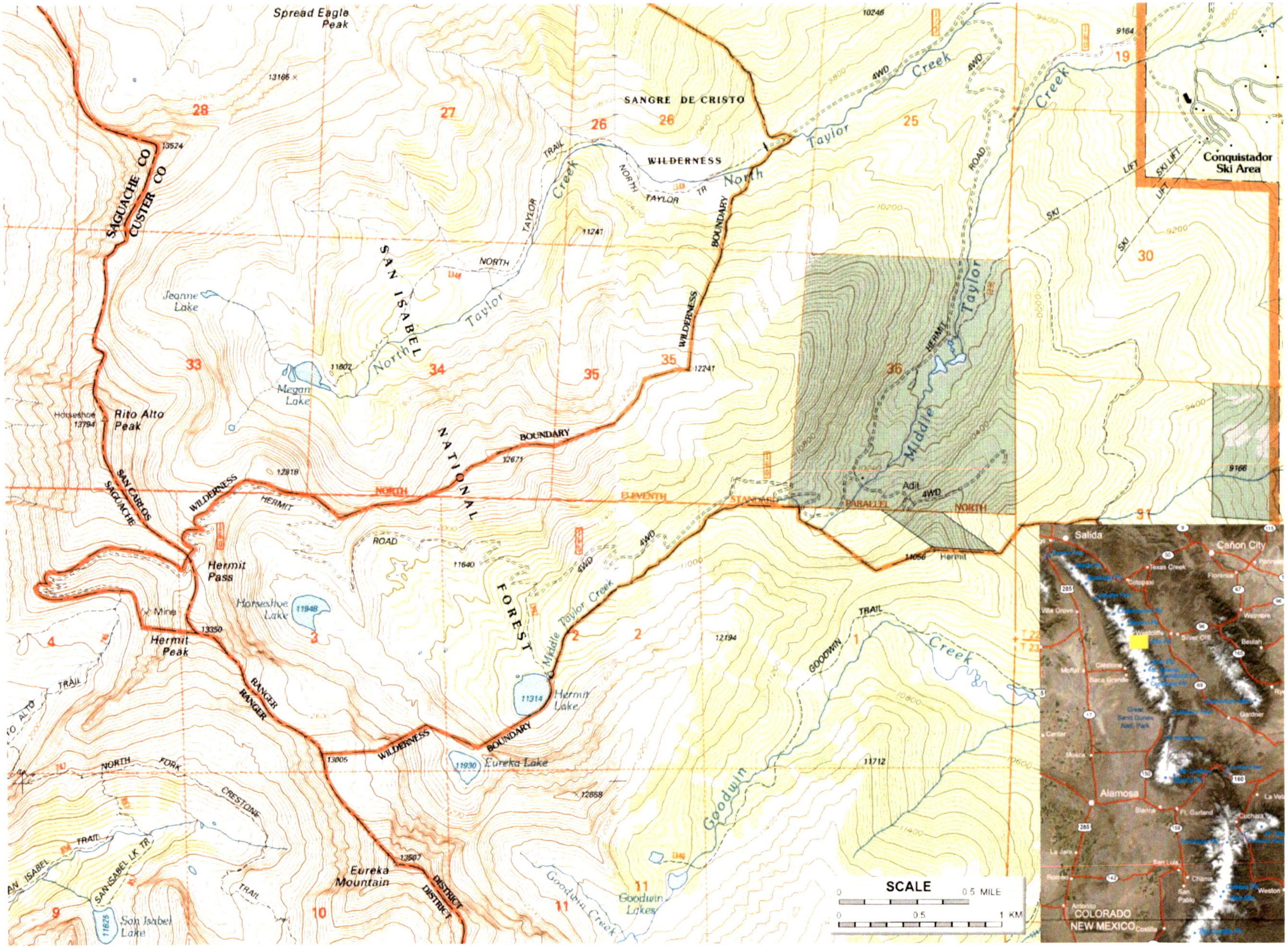

Hermit Pass lakes. This is the easiest to reach, deep part of the Central Sangres, if you have a good four-wheel drive vehicle. The road is closed at the Hermit Pass (13,045'). It is about 0.7-mile hike between the Horseshoe and Eureka Lakes, mostly through the rocks (no trail but very little elevation change), but fishermen say it's worth the effort.

Hermit Ponds (11,790'), view from the southwest.

Middle Taylor Creek Valley Lakes, view from the east. If you hate driving on such a poor quality road, you would need to walk about 8 miles to Hermit Pass from where the Hermit Pass Road is in good enough condition for non-4-wheel-drive cars. It would be a strenuous hike with over 4000' elevation change.

Hermit Lake (11,314') and Eureka Lake (11,930') above it. A relatively flat Hermit Lake Spur Trail connects Hermit Pass Road with the Lake, and it is about a quarter of a mile long.

Colors of the lakes water. The Hermit Lake is deep blue, and the Eureka Lake is more green due a difference in mineral content. The Hermit Pass Road is visible in the top left.

Horseshoe Lake (11,948'). The Hermit Lake is on the top right. Hermit Ponds are on the left. This photo was taken from the Hermit Pass Road.

Megan Lake (11,540') at the bottom, and Jeanne Lake (12,050') on the right, are below the Rito Alto Peak in the North Taylor Creek Valley. Hermit Peak is at the top left.

Megan Lake (11,540'), view from the west. The pond above the Megan Lake (bottom on the photo) is at an elevation of 12,180'.

The entire North Taylor Creek Valley seen from the west. The small and shallow Jeanne Lake is on the left. Hermit Pass Road is on the right. From Gibson Creek Trailhead to Megan lake is 5 miles and vertical 2400', but from the Hermit Pass Road, visible on the right, it is ten times closer and only 1000' down.

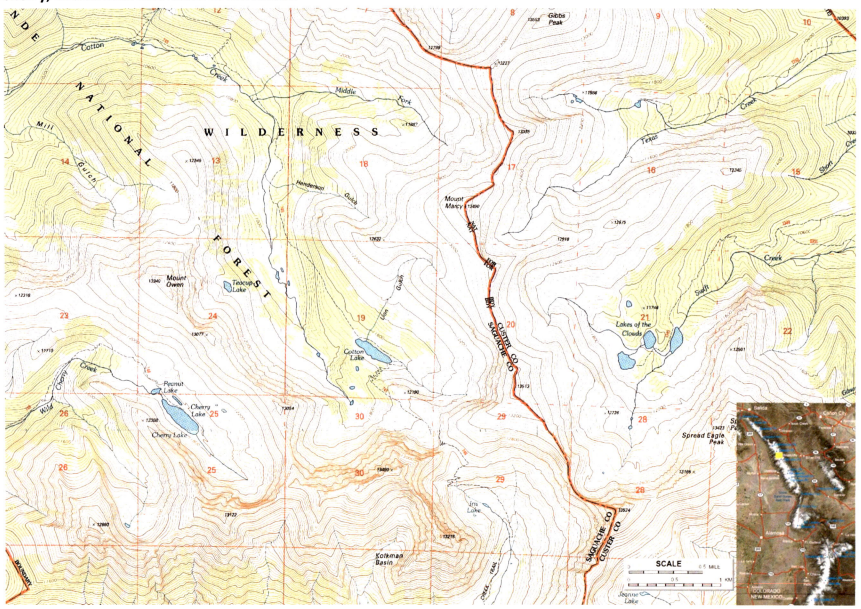

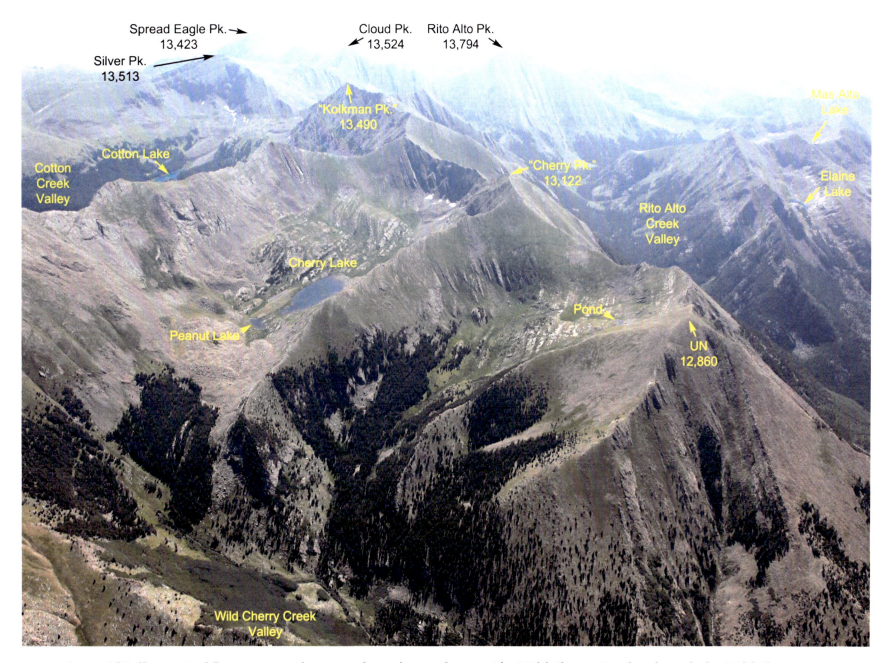

Mount Owen / "Kolkman Peak" mountain ridge, view from the northwest. The Wild Cherry Road ends with the Wild Cherry Trailhead, from which you may start your 6-mile hike (vertical climb of 3300') to the Cherry Lake.

Cherry Lake in the Wild Cherry Creek Valley, view from the south. The Peanut Lake is a small oval-shape lake behind it. Teacup Lake, on the other side of Mount Owen, is in the top right.

Cherry Lake (11,780') and the small Peanut Lake (11,760') below, view from the north. Several smaller ponds are also visible. The highest one, in the top left, is at an elevation of 11,950'.

Mount Owen and "Kolkman Peak", view from the north. All the major lakes of the area are visible.

Teacup Lake (11,750'). Small but very picturesque.

Cotton Creek Valley, view from the south, with Cotton Lake (11,510') and Teacup Lake (11,750') on the east-facing slope of Mount Owen (13,340'). There is a strenuous 8-mile trail with a 4200' climb from the Cotton Creek Trailhead (end of the Cotton Creek Road, on the west side of the Sangres).

Cotton Lake (11,510'), view from the east.

Cotton Lake, view from the northeast, with "Kolkman Peak" (13,490') behind it.

On the southeast slope of the "Kolkman Peak" there are three shallow ponds (see the arrows). The largest got official name Iris Lake (11,890'). Photo made in October. The lower insert shows the Mt. Owen / "Kolkman Peak" mountain group on the left and Silver Peak / Mount Marcy on the right, with the Cotton Creek Valley in between. The top insert is the Iris Lake photo. The Lake is on the Cotton Creek Trail connecting Rito Alto Lake and Cotton Lakes.

General view of the Sangres starting from the Swift Creek Valley. Far in the south: Horn Peak, the Crestones and Blanca Massif. Closer to the Lakes of the Clouds: Spread Eagle, Cloud and Silver Peaks.

Lakes of the Clouds, view from the north. The lakes are very popular amongst the locals.

Lakes of the Clouds, a southwestern view from the ground. There is about a five mile-long trail (vertically 2500') from the Gibson Creek Trailhead to the Upper Lake.

View from the east on the Swift Creek Valley. Spread Eagle Peak is on the left (summit not shown). Cloud Peak ends the valley in the southwest, and the Silver Peak in the west. Mount Marcy ends the Texas Creek Valley in the west. Behind these valleys there are Gibson/Alto Peaks mountain group with Elaine and Rito Alto Lakes, and "Kolkman Peak"/Mount Owen group with Cherry and Cotton Lakes.

Lower (left, 11,470') and Middle (right, 11,580') Lakes of the Clouds.

Middle Lake of the Clouds (right) and the ponds. The largest pond on the left is at an elevation of 11,710'.

Upper and Middle Lakes of the Clouds (11,630' and 11,580', respectively). The arrows in the left point to the top ponds (12,030' and 12,060').

Lakes of the Clouds, view from the east.

Lakes near Gibbs and Electric Peaks

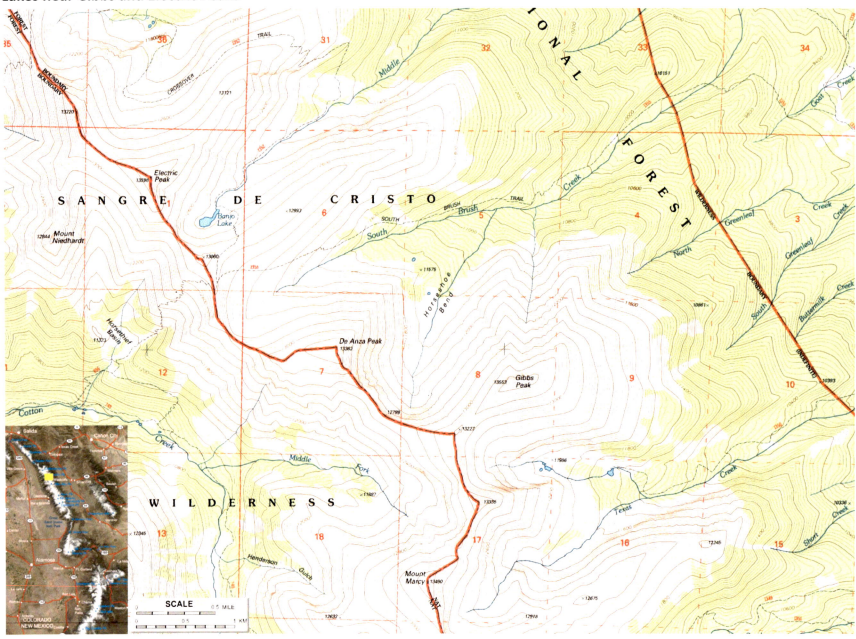

In the Texas Creek Valley there are 3 small lakes (Gibbs Lakes), indicated by arrows. The top Gibbs Lake is at an elevation of 11,950'. Gibbs Peak is on the right. This wide panorama is showing the Lakes of the Clouds, Silver Peak, and Mount Marcy. Behind this mountain chain there is "Kolkman Peak"/Mount Owen mountain group. The Cotton Creek starts from the Cotton Lake, somewhere behind the Silver Peak.

The bottom two Gibbs Lakes (11,380' and 11,420'), and the top Gibbs Lake (right, 11,950'). Starting from Gibson Creek Trailhead it is 7 miles to the largest, Middle Lake (vertical 2300'), and another 0.3 miles to the Top Lake. The Top Lake is not attractive as much as the view on the Wet Mountains Valley from it, not to mention the spectacular wall of Gibbs Peak.

Banjo Lake (12,390') is to the left (south) of Electric Peak (13,598'), in the Middle Brush Creek Valley. There is no trail passing though this valley, but there is access from the South Brush Creek Trail on the left side of the mountain. The Crossover Trail passing through Electric Peak would be another alternative.

When full of water the Banjo Lake shape resembles a banjo (August photo). Electric Peak is on the right. In October (insert) it partially dries up.

Lakes near the Lakes Peak and Cottonwood Peak

South Branch Lake with the southeast side of Lakes Peak, on the right. The South Branch of the North Brush Creek is in this valley. You can get there by a 1.5-mile hike (500' uphill and 800' downhill) from the Upper Brush Lake through the Crossover Trail.

South Branch Lake (11,540'), view from the southwest.

Brush Lakes (11,404' and 11,550') in June. The North Brush Creek Valley is surrounded exclusively by the Lakes Peak (Thirsty Peak technically should be a part of the Lakes Peak due to lower than 300' prominence). The East ridge of the Thirsty Peak splits into two ridges making the South Creek drainage. The northeast part of this ridge becomes the Eagle Peak.

200

View on the Brush Lakes from the southwest. The small top lake is at an elevation of 11,990'. There is no formal name for it, but could be called the Top Brush Lake.

View on the Brush Lakes from the west.

View from the east showing the Lower Brush Pond (10,900'), magnified on the right, and the Brush Lakes at the end of the valley. The standard trail from Duckett Creek Trailhead to the Upper Brush Lake is 6.5 miles long (vertically 2800'), but you may access the Lakes through the Road 331, park your car at its south end, and walk 4 miles: 200' downhill followed by a 1600' climb (see p. 197).

Lower Brush Lake (11,404').

Upper Brush Lake (11,550').

South Lake Creek begins at the South Lake (11,290'), below Eagle Peak. A magnified lake photo is shown in the insert. Thirsty, "4K", and Cottonwood (summit cropped out) Peaks are in the back. Eagle Peak (13,205') is the major mountain in the front, taking most of this photo space. There is no trail that runs through this valley.

Cloverdale Basin (left). The valley is surrounded by the Eagle Peak from the south (left), "4K Peak" and Cottonwood Peak from the west (back), and Wulsten Baldy from the north (right). The photo on the right shows the Balman Reservoir (9404') that is on the road to the Rainbow Lake. The road continues beyond Silver Lake, but its quality is very poor. The access to this road is through the Rainbow Trail Camp (Road 198). From the Camp to Balman Reservoir there is about 2 miles of a rough road.

Rainbow Lake (10, 450'), view from the east. It is about 2 miles from Balman Reservoir, and the road continues another 2 miles to the Cloverdale Basin and Silver Lake Trailhead. There is a 6 mile trail around Cloverdale Basin, passing through the Lake and leading through the Cottonwood Peak / "4K Peak" ridge.

Silver Lake (11,980').

View from the west on Cloverdale Basin with Silver and Rainbow Lakes. There are numerous ponds in it. The Top Pond is as high as 12,390'. The Wulsten Baldy's ridge leads to the Cottonwood Peak (bottom left, summit not visible). Than, the "4K Peak" joins Thirsty Peak and the ridge splits and continues to the Eagle Pk. (east) and to the Lakes Peak (south).

Rainbow Lake (10, 450') and Balman Reservoir (top right, 9,424'), view from the west.

Southwest end of Cloverdale Basin. Brush Lakes are behind the Thirsty-Eagle Peaks ridge.

The most impressive side of Eagle Peak, and several ponds below this mountain.

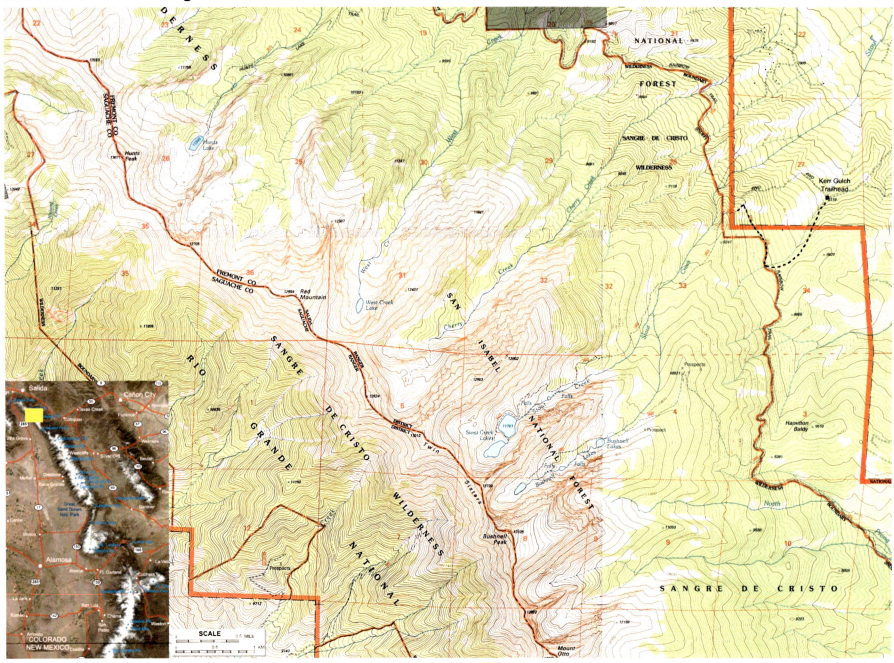

The Bushnell Lakes (11,150', 11,540' and 11,910'), marked with arrows in the center, lay between Bushnell Peak and the Lower Peak of Twin Sisters, that technically belongs to Bushnell Peak because of the low prominence (220'). The Stout Creek Lakes are in the adjacent valley to the north, and the arrow on the right points to the Stout Creek Pond. Late June photo.

Bushnell (left) and Stout Creek Lakes (right), view from the east. The Stout Creek Valley is surrounded by the two uneven mountains called ironically Twin Sisters. Bushnell Peak is the highest mountain of the North Sangres, and with its 13,105' elevation it is only 6 meters shy of 4,000 m.

Stout Creek and Bushnell Lakes, view from the west. The trail to Bushnell Lakes begins at the Hayden Creek Trailhead, near Rainbow Trail, and continues north through Rainbow Trail 2.5 miles to Bushnell Lakes Trail. The total distance to the Upper Bushnell Lake is 5.2 miles (elevation change 2500').

Views from the ground. Top: Lower Stout Creek Lake. Bottom: Stout Creek Pond with a great place to camp nearby. The trail to Stout Creek Lakes starts at the Kerr Gulch Trailhead. It is tricky to choose the right path (see the fix of the USGS map on p. 214, and do not use a 4WD road marked there).

East view on the Stout Creek Lakes (11,761' and 11,860'). The insert shows the Lower Lake and the Pond (11,270'). The trail from the Kerr Gulch Trailhead to the Upper Stout Creek Lake is strenuous and about 5 miles long, with a large elevation gain of 3600'.

View of the North Sangres, extending from Mount Otto (12,865') in the south to Red Mountain (12,994') in the north. The Stout Creek Lakes are in the center. Bushnell Lakes are visible as well.

View from the west on the Stout Creek Lakes and Stout Creek Pond.

West Creek Lake (11,660'). The Red Mountain (12,994') is on the right and the UN 12,924' is on the left edge of the photo.

West Creek Lake, a close-up view, similar to the previous photo. Although there are nice colorful rock formations and great views from this lake, there is no trail that leads to it.

West Creek Lake, view from the west.

Hunts Lake (11,345') in October, view from the east. The Hunts Peak (13,071') is the tallest mountain on this photo, northernmost 13er of the Sangres. The official trail to Hunts lake starts at Bear Creek Trailhead. It is at least 9 miles long (elevation difference is 2400', but with additional 500' up- and downhill).

View from the west on the Hunts Lake.

A wide view on the eastern slopes of the North Sangres near Hunts Peak (bottom right). Southeast direction.

Explanation of Mountain Names

Mount Adams 13,931		Mountain name (with a height in feet given below).
UN 12,873		Unnamed by the U.S.G.S. peak with a prominence over 300 feet.
"4K Peak" 13,123		Unnamed by the U.S.G.S. peak with a prominence over 300 feet and the proposed name.
12,751		A sub-summit of a higher mountain (with prominence under 300 feet)

The prominence of a mountain is the minimal vertical drop from its summit before the slope ascends into a higher peak. In Colorado, the generally accepted criterion for inclusion on lists of independent mountains is 300' of prominence. The 300' rule is sometimes referred to as the Colorado rule (www.peaklist.org). There are several exceptions to this rule because U.S. Geographical Survey Board does not recognize it. Here is a sample list of such exceptions only in Colorado Sangres: Hamilton Peak (13,658' or Blanca Peak B), Iron Nipple (13,480' or UN 13,828' Peak C; UN 13,828' is called unofficially "Huerfano Peak"), Miranda Peak (13,468' or UN 13565' Peak B), Mount Maxwell (13,335', or Marquita Peak B), Thirsty Peak (13,213' or Lakes Peak B), Carbonate Mountain (12,308' or UN 12,330' Peak B), Blizzardine Peak (11,910' or Blueberry Peak B). As you can see, even in this small group of examples, three higher parent mountains have not even been officially named.

References

The lengths of most of the trails described in this book are from: Jason Moore (2003) "Hiking Colorado's Sangre de Cristo Wilderness", Morris Book Publishing, LLC, ISBN 978 0762711086.

Geographical names that were not found on the U.S.G.S. maps were taken from:
1. Kent Schulte (2009) Sky Terrain Trail Map: Sangre de Cristo Great Sand Dunes, ISBN 0966550838.
2. National Geographic Maps (2004): Sangre de Cristo Mountains, ISBN 978 1566953511.
3. Found on various web sites, or created, based on the U.S.G.S. sanctioned name of the nearest relevant feature.

The elevations above the sea level data were from the U.S. Geological Survey TOPO 7.5-minute maps, www.store.usgs.gov.

Index

Most images presented in this book are available in a high-resolution format for printing poster size, high quality photographs. For more photos (also in 3D) and the other publications about the Sangres please visit the author's web site, **www.PikesPeakPhoto.com**